FEB 20 2020

The Sun and Animals

Joanne Mattern

Cavendish
Square
New York

Published in 2020 by Cavendish Square Publishing, LLC

243 5th Avenue, Suite 136, New York, NY 10016
Copyright © 2020 by Cavendish Square Publishing, LLC

First Edition

Website: cavendishsq.com

This publication represents the opinions and views of the author based on his or her personal experience, knowledge, and
research. The information in this book serves as a general guide only. The author and publisher have used their best efforts in
preparing this book and disclaim liability rising directly or indirectly from the use and application of this book.

All websites were available and accurate when this book was sent to press.

Library of Congress Cataloging-in-Publication Data

Names: Mattern, Joanne, 1963- author.
Title: The sun and animals / Joanne Mattern.
Description: New York : Cavendish Square, 2020. | Series: The power of the sun |
Audience: Grades 2-5. | Includes bibliographical references and index.
Identifiers: LCCN 2018048009 (print) | LCCN 2018050322 (ebook) |
ISBN 9781502646651 (ebook) | ISBN 9781502646644 (library bound) |
ISBN 9781502646620 (paperback) | ISBN 9781502646637 (6 pack)
Subjects: LCSH: Light--Physiological effect--Juvenile literature. |
Animals--Effect of light on--Juvenile literature. |
Animals--Effect of temperature on--Juvenile literature. |
Temperature--Physiological effect--Juvenile literature. | Sun--Juvenile literature.
Classification: LCC QP82.2.L5 (ebook) | LCC QP82.2.L5 M38 2020 (print) |
DDC 591.7--dc23
LC record available at https://lccn.loc.gov/2018048009

Editorial Director: David McNamara
Editor: Jodyanne Benson
Copy Editor: Nathan Heidelberger
Associate Art Director: Alan Sliwinski
Designer: Jessica Nevins
Production Coordinator: Karol Szymczuk
Photo Research: J8 Media

The photographs in this book are used by permission and through the courtesy of: Cover Jacob 09/Shutterstock.com;
p.3 (used throughout) Black Prometheus/Shutterstock.com; p. 4 Cesar Deutschmann/EyeEm/Getty Images; p. 6 Sunny Studio/
Shutterstock.com; p. 7 EB Adventure Photography/Shutterstock.com; p. 8 Josiane St Pierre/Getty Images; p. 9 RapidEye/Getty
Images; p. 10 Walter Zerla/Cultura/Getty Images; p. 13 (left to right) ArTDi101/Shutterstock.com, Joseph Mcewan/EyeEm/Getty
Images, Graham Manson/ Getty Images; p. 14 NoPainNoGain/Shutterstock.com; p. 16 Katoosha/Shutterstock.com; p. 18 Janusz Kol/
Shutterstock.com; p. 19 V J Matthew/Shutterstock.com; p. 20 Matt Meadows/ Getty Images; p. 21 Ozerov Alexander/Shutterstock.
com; p. 22 Per-Gunnar Ostby/Getty Images; p. 23 Joe Shelly/Shutterstock.com; p. 24 Gulei Ivan/Shutterstock.com; p. 26 Marten
House/Shutterstock.com; p. 27 Geoffrey Kuchera/Shutterstock.com; p. 28 Volvox volvox/Getty Images.

Printed in the United States of America

Contents

Many animals like feeling the sun's warmth on their bodies.

Chapter 1

Animals Need the Sun

THINK of all the things we need to live on Earth. We need water, food, and air. We also need light and heat. The sun gives light and heat to Earth. Without the sun, nothing on Earth could survive. Without the sun, our planet would be a dark, cold, lifeless place.

A Close Neighbor

The sun is a star. All stars give off light. Because the sun is close to us, its light is bright and strong. That light creates daytime and gives

Swimming helps us cool off in the hot summer sun.

animals and people the light they need to find food and perform other tasks. The path of Earth around the sun also creates the seasons. The sun shines more directly on Earth in the summer, which makes the days longer and hotter. In the winter, days are shorter and colder because the sun's light is less direct.

SUN POWER
It takes about eight minutes for the sun's light to reach Earth.

The sun sets early in winter because Earth tilts away from the sun.

The sun also gives off heat. That heat warms Earth. It makes it possible for animals to survive. Some animals cannot control their body temperature. They need the sun's warmth to stay alive. Even animals that can control their body temperature would freeze to death without the heat

SUN POWER
The sun is just one of millions of stars, but it looks like a large ball because it is the closest to Earth.

of the sun to help them stay warm.

Creating Food

Without the sun, there would not be any food for creatures on Earth to eat. The sun provides the warmth and light that plants need to grow. Even more important, plants can change the sun's energy into food. Animals eat plants, and other animals eat those animals. Without the sun, nothing could survive.

The sun provides energy to plants. Plants provide food for animals.

Sun Worship

Long ago, many cultures worshipped the sun. They knew that the sun created life on Earth, so they thought the sun was a god. One culture that worshipped the sun was the Aztecs. They lived in what is now Mexico. The Aztecs called themselves "People of the Sun." They performed special rituals every morning so that the sun would rise and warm Earth.

Aztecs worshipped the sun. Aztec art often showed the sun.

Young sunflowers follow the sun. Once sunflowers are mature, they only face east.

Chapter 2

Night and Day

ANIMALS need the sun for food. Plants use the sun to make food. Then animals eat plants. Other animals eat those animals and then are eaten by even more animals. This process is called a food chain, and the sun is the part that sets the chain into action.

From Sun to Plant

Plants need the sun's light to make food. This process is called **photosynthesis**. During photosynthesis, sunlight is absorbed by a green chemical in the plant's leaves. This chemical is called **chlorophyll**. It's what gives leaves their green color. The chlorophyll combines the sun's energy with water in the leaves. This creates food for the plants. Photosynthesis also lets plants give off oxygen into the air. Without this oxygen, people and animals would not be able to breathe.

A Day in the Sun

The sun rises in the morning. Its light shines on plants all over the world. These plants include trees, grass, and flowers. The chlorophyll in their leaves gets busy creating food.

Later in the morning, a rabbit comes along. A rabbit is an **herbivore**. The rabbit starts to eat the grass. Other herbivores, like chipmunks, deer, and insects, are also eating plants.

Food chains include both plants and animals.

The rabbit is warm and happy in the sun. But trouble is near. A fox is watching the rabbit. It runs out of the bushes and catches the rabbit. Now the rabbit is food for the fox. This is another link in the food chain.

The fox is not safe either. In the afternoon, a big cat called a lynx spots the fox. The lynx is a **carnivore**. It eats other animals. Now it is going

SUN POWER
Animals that hunt at night need the sun's light and warmth during the day.

Food Chains Around the World

Every animal is part of a food chain. A food chain always starts with plants, who make their own food using sunlight. Plants are eaten by many different animals. These animals, in turn, are **prey** for other animals. Animals that eat a small animal can, in turn, be eaten by a bigger **predator**. Only the top predator in a food chain is not likely to be eaten by another animal.

Every habitat has its own food chain because different animals live in different places. A desert food chain might look like this: Insects, such as beetles, eat a cactus. A prairie dog eats

Food chains begin with energy from the sun.

the insects. A rattlesnake eats the prairie dog. The rattlesnake is eaten by a coyote.

The Sun and Animals

to eat the fox for its dinner. Later, a grizzly bear might eat the lynx.

In the evening, the sun goes down. Now it is dark. But animals are still part of the food chain. Owls, bats, and coyotes are all active at night. They eat animals that got energy and food from the sun during the day. The food chain starts with the sun, but it goes on all day and night.

☀▶ ACTIVITY: Create Different Food Chains

Visit your library to research food chains in different habitats, such as mountain, woodland, swamp, desert, and polar regions. Create a food chain diagram for one or more of these habitats. Be sure to include photos or drawings of each member of the food chain in your chart. Choose how you would like to display your food chains. For example, you might use a poster, a series of index cards, or a PowerPoint presentation. Try to include a fact about each animal or plant or its place in the chain.

This cold-blooded lizard needs the sun's heat to stay alive.

Chapter 3

Hot and Cold

THE sun is not just important because it helps plants create food. The sun's light also powers our days and our seasons. The sun's warmth provides the heat we need to survive.

Staying Warm

Animals need the sun's warmth. Some animals are cold-blooded. They cannot control their body temperature. When an animal needs to warm up, it has to find a heat source. For most animals, this means lying in the sun. As they lie in the sun, the animals soak up the sun's warmth. Their bodies warm up as they absorb the sun's heat. The animal's body temperature goes up.

Staying in the sun can be dangerous for a cold-blooded animal. If an animal gets too hot, it will need to get out of the sun. Many animals cool off by lying in the shade. Some go underground to get away from the sun's warmth. Others cool off in water.

If frogs get too hot, they can cool off in the water.

Warm-blooded animals can control their body temperature. But they still need the sun's heat to stay alive. If the temperature drops too much, warm-blooded animals

A fox's thick fur helps it keep warm in the winter.

have to find ways to stay warm. Some grow thick fur in the winter. Others find shelter in a warm place, such as inside a building.

Changing Seasons

SUN POWER
Sunlight is a source of vitamin D for people and animals.

The light and heat from the sun are not the same all year long. That is because Earth tilts as it spins around the sun. Sometimes Earth is tilted toward the sun.

Then we have hot, bright summer weather. Sometimes Earth tilts away from the sun. Then we have the shorter, colder days of winter.

The change in seasons affects plants, animals, and people. Many plants stop growing during the winter. That means there might not be enough food for herbivores. The lack of sun sends a signal to animals. It is time to plan for winter. Many insects lay eggs and then die. They cannot survive the cold weather. Other insects go underground, where

Cold-blooded snakes curl up together to keep warm.

The Sun and Animals

Changes in the sun's power tell birds it is time to fly south for the winter.

they are protected from winter's cold and snow. Cold-blooded animals like frogs, snakes, and lizards also go underground to stay alive.

The change in sunlight sends a signal to warm-blooded animals. Some **migrate**, or travel to a warmer place for the winter. As the days get shorter and the sun's light gets weaker, these animals know it is time to move on. Later, as the season changes from winter to spring, these animals know

SUN POWER
Too much sun can be dangerous. It can cause an animal to dry out or get burned.

A squirrel stores food for the long winter.

it is time for them to go back to their homes.

Other animals **hibernate**, or sleep through the winter. They find a warm, safe place and go into a deep sleep. Some animals move into buildings to stay warm. Animals that stay active gather food to get them through the winter. They know it is time to do this because the sun is getting weaker.

 ACTIVITY: Winter Predictions

Choose six different animals that live in a cold part of Earth (insects, reptiles, mammals, birds, etc.). Research how each one prepares for winter. Create a poster with three columns labeled Migrate, Hibernate, and Stay. Draw or print a picture of each animal and place it in the column that describes how it behaves in the winter.

The Sun and Animals

Artificial Light

Not all light comes from the sun. Some light is artificial, or created by people. Artificial light includes streetlights, car headlights, and lights in stores and homes. Artificial light can confuse animals. These animals might wake up earlier. Their bodies might think it is time to lay eggs because artificial light makes the sky brighter. However, not all artificial light is bad. Some kinds of artificial light help plants grow bigger and faster.

Many animals, like this owl, need the dark night sky for hunting and mating.

The sun lights our world and provides energy for plants to grow.

Chapter 4

The Sun's Energy and Animals

WITHOUT the sun, nothing on Earth could survive. The sun drives food chains all over the planet. Without the sun's energy, plants and animals would not have the food they need to survive.

A Cold, Dark World

The sun's energy is important in other ways. Without the sun's light and heat, Earth would be dark and cold. No animals could survive without the sun's heat. Earth would freeze, and everything living would die.

Sun Patterns

The sun also creates a pattern that all living things follow. The path of Earth around the sun creates our seasons. Animals know that it will be darker and colder in the winter. When spring comes, the days get longer and warmer. Animals know it is time to lay eggs and have babies.

Birds lay eggs once the sun gets stronger in the spring.

The Sun and Animals

Bears sleep through the winter in safe, warm places.

During the hot, bright summer months, animals raise their babies. There is food to eat. Soon the days will grow shorter and cooler. Fall is coming. For some animals, it is time to migrate or hibernate. For others, it is time to get ready for winter by growing warm fur and gathering food. All of these actions are powered by the sun.

SUN POWER
If the sun went out, everything on Earth would freeze in a few days.

SUN POWER
Vents in the
ocean floor
give off heat
from deep
inside Earth.

Deep and Dark

What about animals that live
deep in the ocean? Scientists
have found some animals living so
deep in the ocean that it is dark
all the time. Instead of the sun, they get
energy from sources such as vents, or gaps,
in Earth's surface. But for almost everything
else on Earth, the sun gives life to animals—
including people!

These crabs live deep in the ocean and far from the sun's light.

Glossary

carnivore An animal that only eats meat.

chlorophyll A chemical in plant leaves that absorbs light.

herbivore An animal that only eats plants.

hibernate To go into a deep sleep during the winter.

migrate To move from one place to another when the season changes.

photosynthesis The process by which plants create food.

predator An animal that hunts and eats other animals.

prey An animal that is eaten by other animals.

Find Out More

Books

Stewart, Melissa. *Beneath the Sun*. Atlanta: Peachtree Publishers, 2014.

Surges, Carol. *Food Chains*. Minneapolis: ABDO Publishing Company, 2014.

Websites

Another Link in the Food Chain

http://www.geography4kids.com/files/land_foodchain.html

Explore the different parts of the food chain and how they all work together, starting with the sun.

The Effect of Sunlight on Animals

https://www.hunker.com/13427960/the-effect-of-sunlight-on-animals-plants

This website describes why the sun is important to all living things.

Index

Page numbers in **boldface** refer to images. Entries in **boldface** are glossary terms.

About the Author

Joanne Mattern is the author of hundreds of nonfiction books for children. Animals are her favorite subjects to write about, along with sports, history, and biography. Mattern lives in New York State with her husband, children, and an assortment of pets.